You
Can Be an Author!

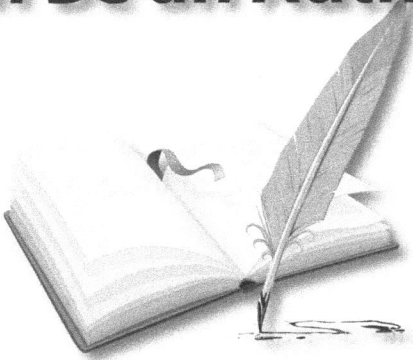

Bettye W. Knighton

Emerge Publishing Group, LLC
Riviera Beach, FL
www.emergepublishers.com

Library of Congress Control Number:
2010942367

ISBN: 978-0-9825699-9-3

Published by
Emerge Publishing Group, LLC
Riviera Beach, FL
www.emergepublishers.com

You Can Be an Author! Bettye Knighton
1. Authorship 2. Self-publishing
3. Authorship-marketing

Editing by Doretha Dennis

Printed in the United States of America

Acknowledgements

Thanks to the members of my focus group:

Margaret Pleasant, Tosha Leake, Alicia Smart, Myrtle Newbold, Nina Brown, Chavela Graham, and Sherrie Core.

Thanks to my inspiration--members of my family:

Husband, Otis; Children: Otis III, Alicia, Tosha, Sonja, and Micheal.

Thanks to my accountability partners--The Palm Beach Life Planners:

Ann McNeill, Sharon Jackson, Stephanie Ebanks, Mariama Williams, Doretha Dennis, Trixy Walker, and Laura Greer.

Dedicated to. . . .

all the first-time authors

who have decided to finally take

that important step

TABLE OF CONTENTS

Part One: Imagine

Part Two: Create

Introduction

I have met tons of people who want to write a book. Writing a book requires skill, motivation and organization. Some future writers have all three qualities, others have one or two. This book is designed to provide you with a basic plan. It will walk you through the maze of bringing your dream to fruition.

I was once where you are today–wondering if I would ever get the book on the inside of me to print. Would I die with the book still inside me?

The biggest library in the world is the cemetery full of unprinted books that no one will ever read. How sad! You do not want this to happen to you.

Most people who have a book inside of them have procrastinated, not because they are lazy, but because they do not know how to get started.

I have learned by trial and error and also from some of the publishing gurus, mainly Gordon Burgett, Dan Poynter, Jason Rich, and Peter Bowerman. These are by no means all of the experts; many more exist out there in the world of writing and publishing.

This book is divided into three sections: Imagine, Create, and Sell. The Imagine section covers the beginning of the book process. This includes making the decision to write a book, what to write about, and what benefits your book can offer the public. What is it that the public may want from your book? What do you want from your book?

In the Create section, we cover the mechanics of writing a book. You must get an ISBN and an LCN number. We walk you through this process. This is the nuts and bolts section.

The third section is the Sell section. It does not matter that you wrote a masterpiece. Who is going to read it if no one knows about it? The book must be marketed. This involves promotion, advertising and fulfillment. It's all about getting your name and your book's name out into the public.

Every idea, project, system or invention begins with imagination. If it can be imagined, it can be created. Once created, it can be sold.

Decide now that procrastination ended the minute you opened this book. From now on, you are on a journey to finally get that book from the inside to the outside. I am with you. Let's go!

Part One
IMAGINE

I can imagine living without food. I cannot imagine living without books.

Alice Foote MacDougall

It's Inexcusable to Die with a Book Inside You

Everyone has a story to tell or information to share. Eighty-one percent of people feel they have a book inside of them. However, only five percent of these people will ever write a book. Many potential authors never realize their calling or gift. They enriched the cemetery with their dead talent. (Pun intended). It truly is inexcusable to leave your story untold and your ideas unshared.

I actively dreamed of writing a book when I was young (in my twenties). When life got in the way, my dream was placed on the back burner. Eventually, it wasn't on the stove anywhere. It had slowly been stomped out of me by a lack of faith in my ability to write and the feeling that my story wasn't worth telling. Nor did I consider myself an expert in any area. I knew a little about a lot of things, but not much about anything.

YOU SHOULD WRITE A BOOK

After being told over and over again, "Bettye, you should write a book", I yielded. There was an incident that spurred me to action. It was nothing earth-shaking, just a simple phone call from a friend. All she wanted was a phone number, but during the course of the conversation she mentioned Professional Speakers Network (PSN). This is an organization of about 150 members, 70 of whom had written books. I was amazed and impressed. I immediately joined; hoping some of that initiative would rub off on me.

After Joining PSN, I was introduced to members of another organization, International Mastermind Association, Inc (IMA). Less than ten months after joining those two organizations, I was the proud author of two books.

MAKE THE DECISION

Once I made the decision to write a book, I realized that I practically had everything I needed in notebooks, binders, folders, and briefcases stored all over the house. Some pieces were even stored on the computer. Over the years I spoke at scholarship luncheons, retirement banquets, graduation ceremonies, women's conferences, workshops, and churches. My first book was a collection of those speeches, devotional lessons, and keynote addresses.

Throughout this book, I will walk you through the process of getting the book from your head to the printed page. Don't worry about a thing. By the time you close the covers of this book, you will be well on your way to becoming a published author. I know you have concerns, but I will address all of them and give you resources for further research.

WRITE AND THEY WILL READ

Even though you have something important to say, you're not sure if anyone wants to listen to you. Why not? People are looking for inspiration, information, entertainment, and tips on how to do just about everything. Are you an expert squirrel catcher? Do you bake the best lemon pound cakes this side of heaven? Can you take a dime and stretch it into a dollar during economic crunch times?

People want to know how you do what you do. You are the expert.

YOUR BOOK WILL HELP SOMEBODY

How many people can be helped by what you have to say? How many lives can be saved by your life story? Can you brighten someone's day with your wit? How about those inspirational poems that are tucked away in a box in the closet? It's time to write that book. Yes, it's inexcusable to die with a book inside you.

You have probably known for a long time that you should write a book. Break the gridlock. Just sit down one day and start writing. I can think of nothing more satisfying than producing a book that is a direct result of the author's heart, soul, talent, and knowledge. It is important to share your ideas, vision, and know-how. There is no acceptable excuse for failing to take action.

Have you ever thought that the technique you discovered to effectively change a C-D student to an A-B student could impact lives? Write a book. Talk about your experience and how you did it. People have inquiring minds; they want to be in the know. Please share your information with the world.

Writing a book requires a lot of effort. Is it worth the time and labor required? Yes, it is. The rewards are significant. Books are timeless. They leave lasting legacies.

You Can Be an Author!

2

What Do Others Want and Expect from Your Book?

Yes, you have a market! Someone is waiting expectantly for your words. Your book will fall into two types of markets: general or niche markets. If you are writing about your experiences with double-dutch jump rope or maybe a handbook on how to produce world champion baton twirlers, you are appealing to a niche market. If you are writing about achieving your life-long dreams, you are appealing to a broader market.

Somebody out there needs to hear what you have to say. There is an audience waiting for your book- no matter what you are writing about! There are markets and distribution channels for your book. We will take a look at a few of them.

There are many reasons people read books. You must determine what is going to draw people to your book. What are they looking for? There are times when I want to be entertained, no heavy stuff. At other times, I am seeking the experts in certain areas that can shed light on a subject and create an "ah-hah" moment for me.

Readers are either looking for information or they want to be entertained. What is your book going to do? Your book is either nonfiction or fiction.

NONFICTION

If you are writing non-fiction, your book will inform. That does not mean you cannot also entertain, challenge or inspire. If you are considering nonfiction, you need to know what the needs are of your audience. What are they looking for? What do they expect? You may be passionate about the mating habits of beetles, but is there an audience for that? Remember, your primary function as an author is to serve your reader's needs.

If you know your field, you already know there is a lot of competition. Do your research thoroughly. There are several resources you may consider:

Library. A very important book available in any library is Bowker's Books in Print. Ask the reference librarian for this book. The books are listed by subject, title and author. There will be a CD version of that book and it may also have several printed volumes. Make a list of the books you would like to review or research. Photocopy the pages you need. Fill your pocket with coins because photocopying is not free.

If you find a number of books in your subject area, make a note of them. This is how you check your competition: Check the copyright dates. Very old books may be out of print. Check with the publishers to see if there is an up-to-date version in print. If not, you have no competition.

Compare prices for books similar to yours. This may be an area where you can gain a competitive edge. If your competition is publishing high-priced, hard cover editions, you can compete by publishing a soft-cover edition with a lesser price. Everyone wants to save money. This could very well be your edge.

Some of the books can be obtained at the library. Others can be purchased at the bookstore or directly from the publisher.

Internet. There is always Amazon.com where you can pick up a used book for very reasonable prices. It doesn't have to be new; all you want is the information. There is also BarnesandNobles.com and other on-line book ordering sites and systems. You can do a Google search on key words to locate books that are in the same category as yours. Invest in a few of these books.

Bookstore. My favorite place to visit is a bookstore. Take a trip to your local bookstore and check the shelves to see what books in your subject are available. It is absolutely necessary to obtain samples to check out your competition and do research.

The bookstores do not have to be stand-alone stores or big chain stores. You can find good deals at Costco or any of the large discount houses. Pay close attention to the title on their display tables. This is a good indication of what kinds of books are in demand. Remember, your objective is to give the readers what they want or expect from a book. They will buy according to their needs.

FICTION. There are over 30,000 manuscripts sent to publishers uninvited every year. Most of them are rejected. However, they do publish a few every year by unknown authors. You could be one of them. You won't know unless you try. If you opt not to go in that direction, we will talk about other options later on in this book.

Children's books. There is an endless supply of books for children under the age of five in the United States. The market for children's books is huge. Conscientious parents are looking for good books for their children to read. Illustration becomes the primary expense when writing books for children. To appeal to young children, the books must be bright, colorful, and well illustrated. Again, search the shelves at the major bookstores and see what's in demand.

Poetry. I am a lover of good poetry, but unfortunately, poetry is not a big seller. You may be able to sell a poem to a magazine for ten or twenty dollars. Some magazines won't even pay that. Instead they will send you a free magazine with your poem in it. But if this your dream, go for it.

Novels. Some of the greatest best sellers of all time have been books of fiction. Some of them are classic and have had great movies made based on them. Some examples are:

- *To Kill A Mockingbird,* Harper Lee
- *The Great Gatsby,* F. Scott Fitzgerald
- *The Color Purple,* Alice Walker
- *Catcher in the Rye,* J. D. Salinger
- *Of Mice and Men,* John Steinbeck

The ultimate objective is to write a book that the public needs or wants. People want to be entertained, informed, inspired and challenged. One or more of these is expected from your book. So, what are you waiting for? Get set, ready, write!

What Do You Want from Your Book?

What's in your eyes, stardust or dollar signs? Some authors want fame; some want fortune. What do you want? Let's take a look at some of the things authors want from their books.

Fame. Hey, why not? Other unknowns have become famous by writing a block-busting, best-selling book. If you think you have the energy required to maintain a high profile, go for it. Some people love anonymity too much to have their privacy invaded;

others want the attention from the media and everybody else. This is your choice.

Riches. Do you want to be rich? If yes, you might want to do something other than writing a book. Riches do not come to everybody who writes a book. Your book is likely to earn money, but the question is—how much?

The Columbia University Study of American Authors compiled the following statistics regarding authors:

five percent of 2,239 writers surveyed earned over $80,000

ten percent earned over $45,000

In addition, the study showed that of the authors who wrote full-time for a living:

28 percent earned $20,000 or more each year

Do not be disheartened. You can make more money on your book by self-publishing. This will call for a greater investment of your time but it will gain four times as much royalty as you would get from mainstream publishing. See chapter six on whether or not to go mainstream or self publish.

Self-satisfaction. Abraham Maslow's "Hierarchy of Needs" scale showed self-actualization as the highest human need. This may be your reason for writing a book–to satisfy a need to be recognized as an accomplished author.

Help Somebody. When you write a "how-to" book, you are helping somebody do something. You are giving valuable information. Even if you are writing fiction, you are either going to entertain or provide a means of enjoyment. Writing fiction offers your audience a period of relaxation.

Example: Patricia Edwards, who had experienced the devastation of cancer in her family, wanted to share with others the questions a woman should ask her doctor regarding breast cancer. Using her expertise as a nurse, she wrote *The Little Pink Purse of Courage*. By writing a book on this topic, she was able to reach many more people through the book than she could through workshops and seminars.

Recording Family History. *Roots* is a book written to record the history of generations of slaves who came to American shores. Although it was written as fiction, it had historical facts expertly woven into the story to give it authenticity and entertainment.

Modern day families are writing family history books. They are tracing their roots back generations and recording them for future generations.

Career Advancement. We have all heard the mantra, "Publish or Perish." College professors have to publish if they want to gain tenure.

You have to decide if you really want to write a book. If the answer is yes, decide why you want to write the book and what you want to write about.

4

It's All in Finding A
Can't-resist Title

"Don't Die On Third" was the title of a speech in the early sixties used in a high school oratorical competition. It's a catchy title that simply means, don't give up. Books are similar. It's all about coming up with a title that will catch someone's attention. You only have about ten seconds to grab the potential reader's attention. If he likes the title, he will flip the book over and check out the back-cover blurb.

USE A FOCUS GROUP

Invest ample time in determining your topic. Use a focus group to help you decide on the final topic. List about ten to fifteen topics and then send them to your focus group. You may have to do two to three rounds before you get a consensus of the top three titles. From the top three titles, you should pick the one you like.

The focus group concept was used to select the title for this book. There were twelve titles and it took three rounds to eliminate nine of them. From the top three, I selected the title. It helps to get input from others. After all, not everyone buying your books will have the same taste you have.

What is the purpose of the title other than giving a hint about the contents of the book? The purpose is to capture the attention of the reader, in hopes of convincing them that your book is worth reading. You have oodles of competition. What better way to gain an advantage than by having a knock-em-dead title.

USE SUBTITLES

Most books have subtitles. This is necessary when the title does not really give a clear indication of what the book is really about. This is especially true in one-word titles or cutesy titles.

Roots - this book by Alex Haley had a simple title. The contents were explained by the subtitle: *Saga of an American Family.*

There are other titles that are five words are less and in some cases, there is no indication of the contents without the subtitle. The subtitle should definitely explain what the book is all about.

Examples:

The Titles

1. *The Call*, Os Guinness

2. *The Parable of the Pipeline*, Burke Hedges

3. *No Matter What,* Lisa Nichols

4. *Like Judgment Day*, Michael O'Orso

5. *One More River to Cross,* Jim Haskins

Now, can you tell from the titles what the books are all about? The titles are catchy and interesting. You may have read one or more of these books because you were able to read the subtitle to get a clue about the contents.

The Subtitles
1. Finding and Fulfilling the Central Purpose of Your Life

2. How Anyone Can Build a Pipeline of Ongoing Residual Income in the New Economy

3. 9 Steps to Living the Life You Love

4. The Ruin and Redemption of a Town Called Rosewood

5. The Stories of Twelve Americans

You get the picture. Without subtitles, you would have no idea what those books were about.

Your title is your book. If you don't believe this, pick up a copy of Dr. Alan Francis's book, entitled *Everything Men Know about Women.* Did people buy it? Yes, they did. However, there was nothing in the book; the pages were blank. They bought it simply for the title.

A good technique in selecting a title is to start with a catchy title and use a subtitle to explain what is in the book. In the process that was used to select a workable title for this book, some of the titles indicated what was in the book even without a subtitle while others would leave the reader guessing.

An excellent example of the importance of a good title is told by the famous Napoleon Hill. He had a book entitled *The Thirteen Steps to Riches.* Admittedly, it was not a box-office title. What he really needed was a million dollar title, a can't-resist title. The publisher asked him to come up with a different title. He tried to the tune of 500 to 600 titles. Nothing worked. The titles just didn't have that can't-resist quality.

Day after day, he tried to come up with a title. Nothing. One day, he received another phone call from his publisher. Mr. Hill was given an ultimatum by his publisher. He told Mr. Hill that if he did not come up with a title by the next day, he was going to give it a title that was totally ridiculous and unacceptable to Mr. Hill.

The book would be called *Use Your Noodle and Get the Boodle.* Napoleon Hill was horrified. That night Mr. Hill commanded his subconscious mind to give him a title. He was talking so loudly to himself that his neighbors thought he was abusing his wife.

Well, 2:00 in the morning, he sat straight up in the bed. "I got it," he said. He called his publisher and gave him the new title: *Think and Grow Rich.* And we know the rest of that story. That book has been translated into hundreds of languages. It remains the basis for many self-help and personal development books. It is one of the best sellers of all time.

The point is it could have remained an obscure book that never got the attention of the masses. That is a lesson for us as we contemplate what title we will use to identify our masterpiece.

Rule of Thumb - Keep your title short and your subtitle longer and more illustrative.

What should you do if you select a title and find it has already been used? Can you use it also? Yes, if you distinguish it by your unique subtitle.

While you have a good idea of your title, it may change during the course of writing your book. If that happens, it's okay. Writing a book is an ever changing process. Your writing may take off in a total different direction than what you started. Just write; let it flow.

5

Who is going to Prep and Write this Gem?

There are authors and there are writers. They are not always one and the same. The author has the idea. The writer has the skills. Sometimes a person may possess both the idea and the skill to put the concept into organized writings.

If you have a brilliant concept for a book, but you flunked English 101, don't worry. Just jot down all your ideas and seek a collaborator. All of the assistance you need to bring an idea to fruition is available. Need an illustrator? You can find one online. Need an editor? There are loads of editors available and some of them are quite good.

Lack of skills cannot hold you back. A good editor can take your poor grammar and turn it into a literary masterpiece. Are your ideas rambling all over the place? You need a collaborator to help you pull your thoughts into an organized manuscript that flows effortlessly.

Collaborator vs. Ghostwriter

Collaborators assist in writing your book; they work with you. There are many reasons you may need assistance. You have valuable information to share, but you just don't have the time to put it all on paper, or perhaps, you don't even like to write. There are celebrities who had a story to tell but didn't have the writing skills to do their story justice.

When do you need a collaborator? You need one if:

- You don't have time to write

- You can't type

- You cannot speak in an organized, precise manner

- You have the ideas, but have difficulty pulling them together

Ghostwriters take on the full responsibility of writing your book. They write for money and not for fame. The ghostwriter's name does not appear on the book like the collaborator's. These ghostwriters are virtually invisible to the readers. They write your book from your notes. Many celebrities use ghostwriters. This can be a lengthy and expensive process.

Normally, ghostwriters deal in autobiographies. Did you ever wonder why so many famous people were also authors? They are not. Ghostwriters to the rescue. They use a process of interviewing to flush out pertinent points that need to be addressed in the book. This can take anywhere from six months to two years.

What do ghostwriters charge? There are two different price structures:

Famous people - Fees are usually 50 percent of the advance and royalties. There is a better than average chance that the book will be picked up by a major publisher.

Non-famous People - Fees can run from a minimum of $10,000 upward to $50,000. It can be more depending on the length and complexity of the book.

Contract writing is another route the author can take. Even less input from the author is required for this method. All the author has to do is provide the subject with some unique ideas and a little direction. Within three months, you are the proud "author" of a book. Of course, it's going to cost you. With contract writing, the manuscript is done from research. The fees can range from $5,000 to $10,000. When the project is complete, the contract writer is gone with no credit given or control over the project. You pay their fee and they're on their way.

Who is going to prep and write this gem? That's totally up to you. You know what options are available to you. What's stopping you? Get moving.

6

Should You Self-Publish or Go Mainstream?

Before you go further into the writing process, you must make a decision: go mainstream or self-publish. This is a choice that is sometimes made for you. Going mainstream is not always an option for emerging authors with no name recognition. Self-publishing may be your only option for your first book. Once your book breaks all records, the big guys will come looking for you.

You have several choices for getting into print. You can approach the "big boys" in New York City or you can try a medium-sized publisher. You can work with an agent or you can go with a vanity press (worse choice). You can make the choice to publish your own book.

Let's take a closer look at some of these choices:

MAINSTREAM
Large Publishing Firms. They are like one-stop shopping centers. You can get everything there—every kind of book and services from A-Z. They publish a variety of books and many topics. They have millions in their audiences.

The firms, sometimes called the Big Six, receive unsolicited manuscripts well into the thousands. If your manuscript is read, consider yourself lucky.

Your manuscript may be rejected even after it is read. But a vast amount of manuscripts are stamped "return to sender" without even being read. To pour your heart and soul into a project that is soundly rejected without being given a fighting chance is heart-breaking. If this happens to you, dust yourself off and try other alternatives.

Medium-sized Publishers. They are smaller, and in some cases, somewhat new to the process. They tend to specialize in certain areas and are sometimes called niche publishers. For example, a book on the mating habits of mosquitoes would be considered a niche book because it only appeals to a small segment of the reading public.

If you're writing a niche book, research the market to determine which publishers work with that genre of books. They have their own distribution system and they can direct your book to its specific market.

I know what you're thinking, probably the same thing I was thinking three years ago. I want to go with the biggest publisher because they are more prestigious. Besides not being able to get my foot in the door, I realized later that medium-sized publishers will sell more books because they sell to bookstores as well as nontrade book accounts.

Vanity or Subsidy Publishers. They will work for you, only if you don't really care about selling to a large audience. You just want to see your name in print. Well, there are some publishers who will oblige you, regardless of the quality of your book. And they will even charge you huge fees to appeal to your vanity.

HOW TO APPROACH A CONVENTIONAL PUBLISHER

If you choose to go mainstream you will need to submit a book proposal if you are writing nonfiction.

If you are writing fiction, you can submit an outline and maybe two or three chapters. If you are submitting a children's book, send the dummy text with suggested artwork.

Writing a book Proposal

Regardless of whether you are going mainstream or self-publishing, it is beneficial to write a book proposal to clarify your thinking.

There are several good resources. The following two are highly recommended:

Write the Perfect Book Proposal:10 That sold and Why (2nd edition), by Jeff Herman & Deborah Levine Herman (Wiley; 2001)

How to Write a Successful Book Proposal in 8 Days or Less, Patricia L Fry (Matilija Press; 2004)

When you submit your proposal to the conventional publisher there are three steps you must take: wait, wait, and wait. If your proposal is accepted, it will still take 18 - 24 months to get the book published. See Appendix C for a sample book proposal outline.

SELF-PUBLISHING

This is not a new concept. It has been around for quite a long time. Some well known self-publishers are Edgar Allen Poe, Rudyard Kipling, Henry David Thoreau, Walt Whitman, and many other great writers.

When you publish your book, you bypass the middleman and deal directly with the printer, graphic artist, and editor. Self-publishing involves an investment of time and money. You do not have to do everything; you act as a general contractor by seeing that the job gets done.

Three Reasons to Self-Publish

1. **Money.** Instead of 6% to 10% in royalties from a publisher, you can have 30% to 40% from your bookstore distributor. If you sell from your website directly to a reader, you can make up to 80% profit. Even with ancillary publishing, you will incur the cost of printing and shipping. Do not overlook your time and overhead.

2. **Speed.** It can take from 18 months to 2 years or more to get your book published traditionally. If you publish the book yourself, you can cut that time by at least 80%.

3. **Control.** There is no guarantee that you can select your title or have a say in the cover design. But when you self-publish, you maintain total control.

Money, speed, and control are not the only good reasons to self-publish. There are tax advantages for author-publishers that are not available for authors. Publishing is a business.

If you decide to build a self-published book, add Dan Poynter's *Self-Publishing Manual* to your library. Read it from cover to cover and you will find everything you need to know about self-publishing.

If your book is a niche book, then my recommendation is Gordon Burgett's *Niche Publishing.* This book is your best guide to publishing in specialized markets. You can get it at the following link:

http://www.1shoppingcart.com/app/?Clk=4043953

You do not have to plead with anyone to publish your book. Do it yourself and enjoy the confidence and self-esteem that comes with being the author of a published book.

Part Two
CREATE

The skill of writing is to create a context in which other people can think.

Edwin Schlossberg

You Can Be an Author!

Organize and Fill up
Your Binder

The first step in your book writing journey is to purchase a three-ring binder. This is going to help you organize your book. There are three sections that you should include in your binder: front matter, the text proper, and the back matter.

Front Matter. In this section you have all of the front book matter such as the title page, copyright page, dedication, acknowledgements, table of contents, preface, foreword, and the introduction.

Text. This is the body of the book, the meaty part. When you determine what you are going to include in each chapter, set the tabs up to match your chapters.

Start your book off with a bang. You want the reader to get past page 18, which is where most book buyers stop if the book is not interesting. Even when you are writing about hard, cold facts, try to keep a light tone. Of course, that may be difficult if you're writing a quantum physics textbook.

Give your chapters interesting names. Some authors repeat the chapter title at the top of the right-hand pages to help the readers find the desired chapters.

Back Matter. Included in this section is your reference material, such as the glossary and other resources. Include an index to help the readers locate specific information in the pages. This is not necessary in a work of fiction.

There is a book-building template in Appendix B that will help you build your book. All of the different parts are listed; you will have no trouble setting up your binder.

The binder should be a 2" model with a clear cover. This will allow you to insert a copy of your book's front and back covers. Setting up a binder is a huge step. The project becomes a living, breathing entity. Now, you have something tangible to confirm that the show is finally on the road.

As you complete a page, use a 3-hole puncher to create some holes and insert it into the proper place in the binder. Now, it's starting to take shape. Before you realize it, you have a rough draft of your book. Don't be overly concerned at this point about choice of words, spelling or making corrections. Just focus on getting the words on paper. The editing and revising will come later.

Do not tuck your binder away into some unseen place. Keep it visible at all times. Every time you think of something to add, just reach for it. Take the binder with you on vacation or on appointments when you have wait time. While you are waiting in the doctor's office, write. When you are waiting for your flight, write. This is a great way to take advantage of time that would be otherwise wasted.

Now that you have organized yourself by setting up your binder, don't you feel better? Your book is now a work in progress.

Designing Your Front and Back Cover

They say you can't judge a book by its cover. That statement is not always accurate. Your cover is just as important as the inside of your book. As a matter of fact, if your cover is not effective, your book will never be purchased or even picked up by a reader. Your title will catch the attention, but the cover layout is equally as important.

I, like most buyers, have a technique for buying a book. When I walk into a bookstore, I peruse the isles in my area of interest. The first thing that attracts my attention is the color of the cover. Strong, vibrant colors catch my eye. You may be attracted by soft, subtle colors. Everyone is different.

The second thing that catches my eye is the title. If I like the title, I will turn the book over and read the back cover copy. If that holds my interest, I will buy the book. Sometimes I will even look at the table of contents, but not always. Let's deal with each item in more detail.

FRONT COVER

Title and Subtitle. The placement of the title is very important. Some books have the author's name in huge print at the top and the title in smaller print near the bottom. You can only get away with this if you are one of the internationally bestselling authors whose name commands attention. Place your title near the top on an uncluttered background so it will be easily seen.

Font. For the front cover, use a font that attracts the attention of the reader, but is not difficult to read. For example, script is very pretty, but is not necessarily effective for a cover. You may have to communicate this to your graphic designer.

Background Colors. You can use light or dark colors for the background, but black is not a good color. Black shows smudges and fingerprints.

Illustration. If you are going to use an illustration, make sure it is professionally done. You can order images from some of the companies that sell rights for the use of images. Some of them are quite good, but be careful. You can select an image that shows up on two or three books. If you have your image done by a professional according to your specifications, you don't have to worry about someone else having your image.

Author's Name. Use a moderate size font for your name. Unless you are already renowned, you want the title to be dominant rather than your name. Don't use "by". Your name is on the cover; everyone knows you are the author. The term *"by"* is used only when someone else is on the cover. For example: Illustrated by Jane Doe; written by John Doe.

SPINE

There is a limited number of books displayed face-out in a bookstore. The majority will be displayed spine-out. This means most of the books on the shelves show the spine and not the face of the book. The lettering on your spine should be easy to read, no script or calligraphy. This is not the place to use fancy fonts.

The largest print on the spine should be the title. Display the author's name and publishing company in smaller print. You do not want anything to detract from the title. Today's technology allows us to stack letters. Make sure that you stack the letters in your title to ensure that it is easier to read without turning your head sideways.

It is always advisable to find out what the competition is doing. Visit the nearest bookstore and locate the section where your book would be displayed. Find the book that captures your attention. Now create what you think would grab your attention from some of those books already displayed. Exercise a little creativity and go for it.

BACK COVER

Description. This is where you need block-busting, eye-catching, killer copy. This is the single most important selling point for your book. If you can't write great copy, it is worth it to hire a professional copywriter. Of course, no one knows your book like you do, so you would have to provide the copywriter with what you think are the greatest benefits of reading your book.

Be careful to stick with an uncluttered look. If your copy is too busy, you will lose the reader before your copy is read. Use white space expertly to ensure that the copy is visually appealing.

Author's Information. Who are you? People want to know. Provide a brief bio including the credentials you have for writing your selected topic.

The Barcode, ISBN, and Price. Every book on the market must have a bar code and an ISBN. The barcode is necessary for retail inventory control and sales. The ISBN is information that identifies the publisher, title, author, and edition. It is normally printed at the lower right corner of the book. Wholesalers, chains, and other bookstores will not accept your book without a bar code.

The price can be imbedded in the barcode but should also be printed in an easily readable font somewhere else on the book other than the top.

Testimonials and/or Reviews. Some authors send out preview copies of their books. They receive reviews back from those carefully selected readers. This gives them the opportunity to get testimonials before the book goes into print. It is helpful if the testimonials are from experts in the field related to your selected topic.

Hiring Professionals to Design Cover

Since the cover is so important, it will be to your benefit to hire someone to do what you are not equipped to do. Hire a graphic designer to design your front cover. You must first give the designer the concept of the book to give them an idea of which direction to take in the design. Do not be hesitant to turn thumbs down on a design you do not like. Sometimes, the designer will give you more than one design to select from.

As a final word on the cover, this is where you pull out all the stops. It would be such a shame if your masterpiece didn't get read because the cover design was weak. This is your competitive edge. Use it masterfully.

9

The Nuts and Bolts of Writing Your Manuscript

Now the real work begins. By now you have done all of your research. You have your winning title, a dynamite cover, and your three-ring binder jam-packed with notes. All right, let's get to it.

You have already zipped off to a good start by doing some of the preliminary work. It is actually your writing system that's the focus here. Now, sit down at your computer and start writing. You are not concerned at this point about creating the perfect manuscript. You are focusing on getting your thoughts and ideas on paper or in the computer.

Today, there is a new book writing model that takes advantage of new technology. We no longer write our books; we build our books. With new technology we can easily insert photos, hyperlinks, artwork and much more. It is like having a professional at your fingertips.

USING YOUR BINDER

You already set up your binder and placed the research and your notes under the proper chapter heading. You can now start inputting your manuscript into the computer. Do not get rid of your binder after you input the chapters. Keep your binder in one place and your hard disk in another. If your computer crashes, you still have a copy of your information. It would also be wise to photocopy your manuscript and put it in a safe place.

Having everything organized in your binder makes your job easier. As you periodically enter changes into the computer, print out the new pages and insert in your binder.

FINDING TIME TO WRITE

What is your most productive time? What part of the day is the best time for exercising your creativity? Some people are morning people; others work better late in the evening. Determine what time is best for you. It is most important to have some consistency. Set aside a certain amount of time daily even if it is just one hour. One well known author takes a couple of weekends at a hotel and finishes his book in two weekends. Of course, at that point he already has an outline and research material.

YOUR WRITING STYLE

Writing is just one form of communicating. Do not over-use big words. Write like you talk. Keep it simple. Your objective is not to impress the reader with your extensive vocabulary. Most people use a small percentage of words available to them. Don't use sentences that are as long as a paragraph, or paragraphs that are a page in length. Books with long sentences and long paragraphs bore the reader. Shorter is better. Follow these tips for a masterful manuscript:

Action Nouns and Verbs. Paint a picture with nouns and verbs that allow the reader to see what you see. A good style to emulate is newspaper writing where the words to be emphasized are at the beginning of the sentence. Each chapter should start off with the main paragraph, while the most important sentence starts off the paragraph.

Proper Terms. Stay away from regional terms, colloquial language and technical language. You do not want to turn the reader off.

Talk on Paper. Even though you have done extensive research, do not fail to put everything into your own words. Words like "which" and "that" are not always necessary and should be left out. You are not getting paid by the word; rather, you are paying by the word. Eliminate junk. Keep it short and simple.

Proper Paragraphs. A good paragraph has a beginning, middle and an end. Each paragraph should have just one topic. The first sentence is the topic sentence.

Accuracy. You are the expert. It is your responsibility to be as accurate as possible. Even in fiction, be realistic in your writing.

FORMAT

Do not use the old double-spaced format. Write in page-layout format. Before you write a single word, set up your margins, header, page numbers, chapter titles, etc. Then fill in the pages. This was helpful for me because I could track the number of pages I had as I went along. If you fail to do this, that

8.5 by 11 format will throw you completely off. At this point you have already determined the size you want your book to be. Unless it is a workbook, 8.5 by 11 will probably not be the size.

TYPESETTING

You have several options in choosing the arrangement of your words for printing. You can hire a book designer/typesetter who knows how to use page-layout programs. You can leave your document in MS-Word. You can also use page-layout programs such as QuarkXPress, InDesign or Page-Maker.

INDEXING

It is important to create an index for a non-fiction book, if you want your book to be taken seriously by the book trade and librarians. Do not struggle with trying to create an index. Let the professionals do it. If you prefer to do it yourself, be prepared to spend 3 or 4 hours on the Index depending on the size of your book.

ADDING VISUALS

A book with visuals is superior to a book with no visuals. Where appropriate, add photographs, bullets, buttons, icons, line drawings and/or cartoons. There is copyright-free art available to you from http://www.ClipArt.com for a low fee.

Photographs. A picture adds clarity to what you are trying to convey. Integrate words and pictures to strengthen your message. If you already have photos, scan and load them into the computer. Then crop, size, and put them into place. You can also import pictures from sites such as fotolia.com, istock.com, and ClipArt.com.

Drawings. Use the same process for inserting drawings into your manuscript. Add a caption to make the image more understandable.

A BINDING DECISION

The standard binding for "trade paperback" books is called "perfect binding." This is how the overwhelming majority of books are bound. What about spiral binding? Well, if you have a book that you want to lie flat when open like a cookbook or work book, then you need an alternative to "perfect" binding. The alternative to perfect binding is spiral binding. There are several kinds of spiral binding:

Comb Binding. This is a plastic comb-type binding. You may see this used on workbooks or cookbooks. The advantage of this type of binding is that it lies flat without tearing pages from the spine. The major disadvantages of comb binding are: no title on the spine, they crush in shipping, and the wire cuts the envelope. Another disadvantage is that sometimes the pages are uneven. This can be expensive if printed in large quantities because often they have to be hand fed into binding machines.

Double Wire-O Binding. This binding has two wires threading each hole. This allows for a more accurate page alignment. This is perfect for personal sales where bookstores are not involved. The disadvantage of this style binding is the same as comb binding. Libraries and bookstores do not like this kind of binding.

Combo Binding. This method combines the best of comb and double wire binding. It has the appearance of "perfect binding" and it lies flat. The disadvantage is that it costs more, but if lying flat is important, it is worth the extra expense.

BOOK LENGTH

Before pricing is considered, think about the size of your book. If the book is too slim you will not be able to command the price you wish. Likewise, if the book is too thick with 600 or 700 pages, it will be too expensive to print and too expensive for the buyer.

Ideally, your book should be between 144 and 288 pages. If your book ends up being less than 100 pages, add some resources. Do not add junk to bulk up the book. Instead, add valuable resources: other books, websites, links, and anything else that will be helpful to the reader. To add length to the book, you can add anecdotes, pictures or use more white space. Paper is the most costly part of the book so you don't want a 900-page book.

Books printed on a web press are assembled in signatures of 48 pages each. Therefore, 144 pages amount to three signatures of 48 pages. Do not let that distract you while you are writing. You can worry about page count when the manuscript is done and ready for typeset.

THE PRICING FORMULA

Keep the price of your book competitive with similar books on the market. Visit the bookstore and check the price of the books of your genre. If there are none in your category, check those books that are closely related to your topic.

There is a formula used by some authors. It is the "6 x PPB" rule. That is six times the cost of the printing per book. If a book cost $2 to print, you can set the price at $12.

THE PRINTER

When it's time to roll the presses, a decision must be made: Traditional offset printing, Print on Demand (POD), or e-books? The method you choose is based on your budget, target audience, goals, distribution, fulfillment, and the quality of book you are aiming for.

Offset Printer. These printers provide high image quality. The production is fast and the per-copy printing cost is lower than other options. The disadvantage lies in the larger upfront investment because you are paying for hundreds or thousands of books being printed at once. Another disadvantage is being responsible for book publishing related tasks that a POD company would handle for you.

Print-On-Demand. This is a popular choice among self-publishers because of its many benefits. POD takes the hassle out of the process of publishing. The biggest benefit is a complete turnkey system that handles the everyday things of the publishing process. This frees you up to do what you do best: *create.*

The POD technology burst on the scene in 1995. Offset printing for those authors who are not signed up with a publishing house could cost as much as $10,000 to $20,000, plus funds to market, promote, and distribute their book. But with POD, you can get all of those services from $300 to $1500.

Do careful research in selecting a POD company. You can use any Internet search engines and the search phrase *Print-On-Demand book publishing.*

PUTTING THE PIECES TOGETHER

All books, whether fiction or non-fiction, contain certain elements. You make the decision about which elements you put in your book based on your personal preferences. Some of these elements are required such as the copyright page. For example, you do not need a dedication or acknowledgement page.

Copyright. This is covered in chapter 10.

Author Acknowledgements. This is where you thank everyone who helped you write and publish the book. You can also thank your loved ones who put up with you while you were preoccupied with the writing of your book. This can be up to a page, but try to keep it within two paragraphs.

Table of Contents. This is simply a list of the chapters and major sections within your book and their respective page numbers in a directory-type listing.

Foreword and/or Preface. A foreword is typically written by someone other than the author. This can be one to five pages and contains information about what's included in the book.

A *preface* contains much of the same information as the foreword does but is usually written by the author. You can have both a preface and foreword, but this practice is not too common. Very seldom does a book have both.

Introduction. The content of the book is introduced here by the author. It can be one page or it can be as long as any of the chapters in the book. This is entirely your choice.

Appendixes. This is found at the end of the book. If there is information that did not easily fit into any of the chapters, you can include it here. Worksheet, charts, graphs, and any other pertinent information can be included in the appendixes. This is also where you will list resources.

Bibliography. For most non-fiction books, other sources are relied on. List them here in a traditional format such as the Chicago annual Style (University of Chicago Press). Visit www.chicagomanualofstyle.org for more information.

Glossary. You may or may not need a glossary. This is a list of terms and their definitions. If your book contains a lot of technical terms, this will be a good reference for your reader. Keep your definitions short.

Index. This is a detailed listing of keywords and topics featured in a non-fiction book. It is more detailed than a table of contents. The index provides a valuable resource for locating specific information within a book. Putting together an index can be time consuming. Most POD companies provide an indexing service for an additional fee.

Author's Bio. Although information is provided on the back cover about the author, it is very brief. On this page, there is more detail given. It can be placed in the front of the book or at the end of the book depending on the author's preference. Also within this section you may choose to promote your Website or your business.

KEEP IT LEGAL

You must obtain permission for material you use in your book that is copyrighted, trademarked, or patented. You don't need permission for short snippets of copyrighted material (a paragraph or less) unless the item itself is very short, like poetry or lyrics. The written permission you obtain can be in the form of a letter with the signature of all involved or a more formal document prepared by a lawyer. Always give credit where credit is due.

THE ORDER BLANK

The reader may want to send a copy of your book to a friend as a gift. Include an order blank on the last page on the left side facing out. Make the ordering process simple for the readers. List the full price of the book including sales tax (if applicable, and shipping.

If readers are going to order using the order blank, you should have the capability to accept credit cards. It is easier to get Paypal for a credit card than a bank card.

You Can Be an Author!

Getting Your ISBN, Copyright, And Library Control Number

ISBN

Every book that is commercially available has an ISBN number. This is part of a book identification system. It was formerly a 10-digit number, but has been upgraded to a 13-digit number. You will see some books with both the ten and the 13 digit numbers.

The numbers are assigned by R. R. Bowker in New Jersey (www.bowker.com). It is not free. (Is anything?) You will pay $275 or more for a block of

10 ISBN numbers. That could change by the time you read this book. Prices only change in one direction and that's up. You can purchase a block of 100 and get a cheaper per unit price. If you think you're going to write a hundred books, go ahead.

Some authors decide to get their numbers from their printers. That's okay, but make sure the ISBN is in your name, not theirs. The ISBN number identifies the "publisher of record." For all books published after October 2007, the 13-digit number is the only one to be used. Include the number on your copyright page as follows:

ISBN-13: 978-2-8777610-0-9

Every version of your book will have a different ISBN number. The hard cover, the soft cover, and the eBook version will have a different number. When you get your log of numbers, it is not necessary to start off in order with the number that ends in 0. Zero signifies to all that this is your first book. I recommend you start somewhere in the middle. After you have a few titles under your belt it doesn't matter about using the first number.

The ISBN-13 has five parts:

The new prefix: A 3-digit number that identifies the book   industry, currently 978 or 979.

Group of country identifier: The section that identifies the country where the book was published.

Publisher identifier: A unique code given to every individual publishing company.

Title Identifier: The part of the ISBN that is unique to every book and identifies the particular title or edition of that title.

Check digit: This single digit at the end of the ISBN validates the number.

When Should You Register for an ISBN?

There are 160 ISBN agencies throughout the world. Each one of them assigns unique ISBNs to new publishers within a specific region of the world. For the United States, we use the U.S. ISBN Agency which also handles Guam, Puerto Rico, and the U. S. Virgin Islands. If you are not self-publishing, the publisher will obtain the ISBN number on your behalf.

If you should decide to self-publish your book, you first need to establish a publishing company. Once you do that, you can apply for a block of ISBN numbers. Contact the U.S. ISBN Agency.

To acquire an ISBN publisher prefix and purchase a block of ISBNs, you must first complete and submit the appropriate form (Application for an ISBN Publisher Prefix) to the U. S. ISBN Agency. You can either apply for it online or via printed form. The online address is:

www.isbn.org/standards/home/isbn/us/secureapp.asp

For printed forms visit:

www.isbn.org/standards/home/isbn/us/printable/isbn.asp

After you've completed the printed forms, send them to:

R.R. Bowker, 630 Central Avenue, New Providence, NJ 07974

Be prepared to supply information about your publishing company. Information to be supplied includes the company/publisher name, the address, contact person, the year the company was founded and started publishing, and the company's primary focus in terms of subject areas covered.

When you have completed that process and obtained your ISBN publisher prefix, you can assign individual ISBNs to your upcoming books. Then you can list each title with Bowker's Books in Print at www.booksinprint.com.

Barcodes

The bar code on a book identifies the ISBN number, which in turn identifies the publisher, title, author, and edition. Bookstores will not accept your book without a bar code. If you send one anyway, they will supply a sticker bar code and charge you for it.

Always print it on the lower half of the back cover on hardcover and soft cover books.

Sample Barcode

ISBN 978-0-9818383-3-5

COPYRIGHT

Your book is automatically copyrighted by virtue of the fact that you created it. That does not mean it can't be contested. If you and someone else come up with the same idea and the other is copyright registered and yours is not, you have a problem. You have come this far. Why not invest the time and finances to protect your work.

The process of getting your masterpiece copyrighted is simple. Visit www.copyright.gov. Under Publications, click Forms. The Short Form, TX is adequate for your needs. Follow the instructions. In the past, a request for two copies was standard; however, you can digitally send in the file and save yourself about $30. Otherwise it will cost you about $65 to send in the actual paper copies. Remember, the push for going green is moving full force.

Copyright Date

A couple of definitions are helpful here. OPD is the "official publication date", the date you announce to the world that your masterpiece is officially released. BBD is the "bound book" date-the date you have your printed books in your hot little hands.

It matters what date you use as your copyright date. If you are close to the end of the year, it is advisable to use the next year's date. There should be at least four months between the OPD and the BBD. It is perfectly alright to sell your books from your website before the official publishing date. You should be so lucky as to sell out your first printing before OPD.

Copyright Notice

The copyright page in all versions of your book should contain three items:

- The copyright symbol-the letter c in a circle © or the word "copyright"

- Your name as owner of the copyright

- The year of first publication

An example of a one-line copyright notice reads: © 2010 Bettye W. Knighton

LIBRARY OF CONGRESS CONTROL NUMBER (LCCN)

This is a number assigned to your book that's used by libraries for numbering and cataloging books. This number was implemented in 1898. Do you want your book to appear in libraries? This is a must-have number. It includes the year of publication and a unique serial number for each book title. It is important that you obtain this number before your book is published so that you can include this number on the copyright page in your book.

This service is free. To acquire your LCCN number, just visit www.pcn.loc.gov, complete the necessary form and mail it to:

Library of Congress, Cataloging in
    Publication division
101 Independence Avenue, S.E.
Washington, D.C. 20540-4320.

You must already have your ISBN to participate in this program.

11

Edit, Revise,
Edit, Revise...

First draft. Second draft. Third draft. Perfection is your goal. So get ready to edit and revise over and over again until you are satisfied. Hopefully, you are getting a second set of eyes to look at your manuscript. There are pesky little editing problems that can escape the best of eyes. You have commas that stand behind the wrong words or periods that are missing in action.

YOUR RESPONSIBILITY AS AUTHOR

First Draft. You may have decided to turn your manuscript over to a professional editor. That's a fantastic idea, but as the author, you still have a responsibility to review your manuscript several times before passing it on to the professionals. In this draft, focus on content. No one knows better than you, what you intended to put in your book.

Second Draft. During this draft take a close look at the quality of your writing. Are your ideas clearly stated? Will it be easy for the reader to understand what you are trying to say? Did you use the best words for conveying your thoughts?

Third Draft. Has all the spelling been corrected? Your software may catch many of the spelling errors and some of the grammatical errors. But it cannot catch instances where you used the wrong word unless you really have a sophisticated editing software package. This is where you have to rein in unruly punctuation marks. They like to show up where they are not needed and hide when they should be holding down the fort.

Fourth Draft. This is where you polish your manuscript. The thoughts are clearly communicated. All spelling and grammatical error have been corrected. The manuscript flows effortlessly. If you are satisfied with the document, fine. But I would recommend allowing another set of eyes to look over the manuscript. You are too close to the project to see everything.

THE EDITOR'S RESPONSIBILITY

Editors check everything: style, syntax, grammar, punctuation and spelling. For example, which word is better suited for your manuscript *honour or honor*? A good editor knows which is best. They have, hopefully, years of experience.

When the editor is finished with your manuscript, you will have to re-read it to make sure your ideas or thoughts were not changed. Editors will make stylistic, substantive and structural changes but they should not change your concept.

REFERENCE BOOKS

There are several books that are very helpful in the editing process. Besides a good dictionary, you should have the books listed below in your library:

The Gregg Reference Manual - This is a book on grammar, style, usage and the formatting of business documents.

A thesaurus or dictionary with synonyms and antonyms.

The Careful Writer: A Modern Guide to English Usage--a book on usage.

WATCH OUT FOR.....

Long Sentences or Paragraphs. I have seen paragraphs that went on for pages and sentences as long as paragraphs that had to be broken up. Review this before you send it to an editor.

Spelling Mistakes. These are not always misspelled words. Sometimes it is a case of using the wrong word, i.e., here for hear or break for brake. I'm not kidding. You see all kinds of errors in the documents. Some words are easily confused because they look alike or sound alike (or both) but have different meanings. The task becomes choosing the correct word.

Factual Errors. Check and re-check your facts. It is a terrible blunder to publish a book with erroneous facts.

Wrong Page Numbers in Table of Contents. Sometimes chapters are deleted or inserted or moved around. Don't forget to change your table of contents. As a matter of fact, don't insert page numbers in your table of contents until the book is complete.

Improper Use of Punctuation. Use your Gregg reference manual to help with this problem.

Grammatical Errors. Again, your Gregg Reference Manual is your best bet for fixing grammatical errors.

Typos. Words that the spelling checker didn't check, for instance, your instead of you're.

COST OF EDITING SERVICES
 Some editors charge a flat rate, while others charge an hourly rate. Others charge by the word, ranging from one cent to five cents.

WHERE TO FIND AN EDITOR
Do you know anyone in the publishing industry who can recommend you to an experienced editor? Or maybe someone who works for a newspaper. If not, there are resources online. Try one of these:

Elance (www.elance.com)
Freelance Work Exchange
   (www.freelanceworkexperience.com)

Manuscript editing
(www.manuscriptediting.com)

We are in the age of hi-tech, so it is not necessary to be located in the same area as the editor. You can communicate via phone, fax, email or teleconference.

PROOFREADING

According to *The Gregg Reference Manual,* there is a difference in proof reading and editing. The book should be proofread before it is sent to the editor. When proofreading a document, watch out for the following types of mistakes.

1. Repeated words (or parts of words) at the end of a line and the beginning of the next line.

   We are looking forward to the release of your new your new publishing book.

2. Substitutions and omissions, especially those that change the meaning.

Original Material	Erroneous Copy
I agree to pay you $55.50 for the bicycle.	I agree to pay you $5560 for the bicycle.

3. Errors in copying key data.

	Original Material	**Erroneous copy**
NAMES:	Bettye J. Walker	Betty J. Walker
TITLES:	Ms. Janis Dobbs	Mrs. Janis Dobbs
DATES:	December 15, 2004	December 15, 2040
PHONE NOS.	561-863-9554	516- 863-5954

4. Transpositions in letters, numbers, and words as well as typographical errors. (These are the kinds of mistakes a spell checker does not usually catch.)

Original Material	**Erroneous Copy**
We have 31 new students for the class starting May 13.	We have 13 new students for the class starting May 31.

5. Errors in spelling and inconsistencies in format (for example, indenting some paragraphs and not others).

Original Material	**Erroneous Material**
Dear Mrs. Fortune: Thank you for your letter of congratulations.	Dear Mrs. Fortune: Thankyou for your letter of congratulations

As a final step in proofreading, check the document for overall appearance. Is each page attractive? Is the format easily readable? When you have completely proofread your book and made the necessary corrections, you can have a second of eyes look at it to catch anything you may have missed.

12

The Professional's Last Step Tools

You can create a book with just a pen and some paper. But in this hi-tech age, there are tools that will make your job easier. These are tools that are essential to your successful publishing venture.

Computers. This is by far, your most important tool. It can be used to search the Internet. It can also be used for writing, typesetting and promotion. Computers are reasonably priced now so buy the best you can afford. With the computer you can easily do all the research for you book project. E-mail is the fastest way to send research questions. If you are working with a collaborator or ghostwriter, this is a great means of communication.

Computer Writing. The benefit of writing using the computer is being able to edit as you go. Misspelled words can be corrected instantly. Some of the software programs will flag grammatical errors. This speeds up the editing process that comes later.

MS Word will mark the revised portions of a document in the margin to indicate the sections that need adjusting. The revision marks are deleted on the final printout. This is helpful when more than one person is working on a manuscript.

Workspace. Your workspace should have excellent lighting. You want to finish your book with your eyesight still intact. Remove as much clutter as possible. Some people can work in the midst of clutter; others can't. Every two or three days, clear your area of excess paper.

Reference Books. You need a good set of reference books. You do not have to purchase them new. You can save money by shopping at used bookstores. Some of the reference books you need are:

The Gregg Reference Manual, A book on grammar, punctuation and style.

A good dictionary.

A thesaurus or dictionary of synonyms and antonyms

The Chicago Manual of Style, 14th edition. This is a stylebook.

Copy Machine. This equipment is not as much in demand as it was before the advent of computers. Now you can go online on your home computer, locate the information and print it on your printer. But it is still good to have a copy machine for those few times when it is absolutely necessary to have one.

Software. There is software on the market that can help you with the editing process. Search on the Internet for editing software. There is also software that will help you design a cover for your book.

Hand Held Recorders. Keep a recorder with you. When a thought comes to mind and you are not in a position to write it down, speak it into the recorder and transcribe it later. There are some excellent ones on the market. Again, go online and put "hand held recorder" into the search engine. You will get a long list to choose from.

Cameras. There are some excellent cameras on the market today. Get a good digital camera. You can use it to download the photos directly into your manuscript. There are also excellent flip video cameras that you can use to load excerpts for videos about your product onto YouTube. This has to be less than 10 minutes.

Machinery. Time is expensive. As you continue writing, you will need labor-saving devices to get the greatest benefit from your efforts. Personal computers, fax machines, mobile phones, and other devices that are constantly hitting the market will be useful. By the time you read this book, there will be other items that will save time and effort.

Part Three
SELL

When you sell a man a book, you don't sell him 12 ounces of paper and ink and glue-you sell him a whole new way of life.

Christopher Morley

13

Promotion

Promote, promote, promote! Writing the book is just the first step. Whether you go with a publisher or you self-publish, you have responsibility for promoting your book. Fantastic! The book is written. It's time for the money to roll in. The main way you measure success is with money. Is there another way? Of course, but you still want to have some money to show for all your efforts.

No matter how good your book is, you must promote it. If you don't have the advantage of having one of the Big Six backing you, it's all up to you.

There a multitude of ways to promote your book. I will list many of them in this section. You do not have to do all of them, but you certainly need to do some of them. Execute the ones you want and discard the others.

The age of technology has affected the manner in which books are promoted. You don't even have to get dressed in the mornings to go out and promote. You don't have to focus on newspapers and magazines; some of them are going out of business, anyway. News media has replaced lots of venues. There will be some overlap with promotion and advertising. But that's okay, as long as the word gets out about your book. Be methodical and persistent. Promotion takes time.

Don't expect your book to automatically sell as if by magic. Unfortunately, it doesn't work like that. I wish it did. The key is to let potential buyers know about your book, so let's take a look at some of the methods of promotion.

Viral Marketing. One person sneezes; ten people catch a cold and spread it to a hundred others. They, in turn, spread it to another thousand. That's the way viral marketing works. This method refers to marketing techniques that use popular social networks to effectively increase brand awareness or to accomplish other objectives. Some people use social networks for just that-socializing. But you must use it for business to increase sales of your book.

Review Copies. This is not very expensive. Reviews cost very little in time and money. The materials required to put together a promotional package can cost as little as $5 or less. You can send review copies to over 100 magazines for less than $500.

Email. Send emails to your colleagues and everybody on your email list. Copy/paste the back copy blurb and send to everyone in your address book. Friends like to help. Use the "Please-help-me" technique. Don't ask them to buy your book; instead request that they forward your email to everyone on their list. This could well become viral.

Online Listings. Review the Resource section of this book for a list of free sites where you can post your book cover image, back cover blurb and link. Some will require you to register with a username and password. Whatever it takes, do it.

Contribute to articles. The fact that you have become an author makes you an expert in your subject area. There are writers and editors looking for information in your subject area. They subscribe to various services. As an author you should subscribe to those same services. I am listing a few of them here:

http://www.PRNewswire.com

http://www.ProofNet.com

http://www.HelpAReporter.com

Sign up and you will be notified when articles are requested in your area of expertise. On the last one listed above, I had the opportunity to be included in an article regarding retirement. It was good exposure in a national online financial newsletter.

Email Signature. While presenting a workshop on writing and publishing, I mentioned email signatures to the audience. One of the participants was astounded that he had missed that method. He stated that he sends out hundreds and hundreds of emails and never once thought to use this method. Email signatures drive traffic to your website where you sell, sell, sell.

An example of an effective signature:

BETTYE W. KNIGHTON
Motivational Speaker

Majestically Speaking

Unlock the Door to Your Success
Contact Me for Conferences, Workshops, etc.

P.O. Box 9135
Riviera Beach, FL 33419
Cell: 561.601.0349

Virtual Book Tours. A virtual tour is just what it says–a book tour that you can conduct in your pajamas from your home or from your office (not in your pajamas!).

News Releases. Your headline must be an absolute block-buster. You have five seconds or less to convince the editor to consider doing your story. Don't send them a book. Keep your copy to four hundred words or less. You are only trying to generate interest in you and your book. In this age of technology, your news release does not have to be just words on a page; it can be video clips, audio files, images, or links to other pages. It is important that you include a picture of the front cover of your book in the release.

Try these online media distribution services:

http://www.Businesswire.com

http://www.PRNewswire.com

http://www.Prweb.com

Your Website. Do you really think you can sell a book without a website? Well, you can't, not effectively anyway. You need a destination to drive the traffic to. Your online presence is of paramount importance to your success online.

Make sure your website is rich in content and not just a "buy now" page. Post information from your book to entice them to buy your book. One-page websites are popular now and sometimes they point to a major website. Your single-page, single-topic website will be picked up by search engines.

Blog Talk Radio. Hi-tech rules the day. In 2006, Blog Talk Radio was launched to the tune of almost two million listeners a month. This service is free. They make their money from advertising. As a user, this system allows you to field phone calls, upload music, run live radio shows. You can even archive your shows. Give this a try. http://www.blogtalkradio.com/

Social Media-Social Networking. We have been social networking for eons. But this kind is different. We are not having coffee klatches; instead we are sharing thoughts, information and ideas via the Internet. People around the world can find you and you can find them.

According to Google, social networking is linking people to each other in some way. Wikipedia says social media can take many forms, including wikis, podcasts, weblogs, Internet forums, video, message boards and pictures. The Internet is our biggest ally. As authors and publishers of non-fiction, it is possible for people to find and interact with people all over the world.

Some of the examples of social media applications are MySpace, Facebook, YouTube, Twitter, Flickr. To get more information on these applications, visit http://en.wikipedia.org/wiki/Socialmedia

You Can Be an Author!

Advertising

Advertising is a part of your overall promotion process. It doesn't do any good to build a better mousetrap if no one knows where to find it. You have to go into overdrive to let the world know you have not just a book, but a must-read book. There are professionals that can help you with advertising copy. Again, everything you need can be located online. Do your research carefully.

A Word of Caution: Before you spend a single copper penny, make use of free publicity.

WEBSITE

The single most important method of advertising is your website. The design of your site is crucial. It needs to be eye-catching. Everything you have in terms of materials, i.e. press-kit materials, books, CD's, DVD's should be listed there.

The Internet is a wonderful tool; you don't have to spend money on envelopes, stuffing, postage or trips to the post office. Email provides feedback so much faster than snail mail. You can send out email blast using companies like Constant Contact, Icontact or Mailchimp. There are many others. In the past, authors sacrificed to print and distribute expensive four-color brochures. That is no longer necessary. Spend a little time and you will save a lot of money.

Get a Universal Resource Locater, commonly called a URL. It is the address of a web page on the world wide web. Your URL should incorporate your company name, your name, and title. Brand identity is important, too. Everything should point to you- business cards, bookmarks, website. Make sure you use the dot extension .com because that is more professional.

TESTIMONIALS

It is always a plus to have testimonials, especially from those who are experts in your chosen field. Some authors send out advanced review copies of their books to carefully selected readers. From the reviews, the author extracts a sentence or two and includes those as testimonials. You can also post these testimonials on your website. Use the short testimonials for emails and your back cover. Save the longer ones for the website.

SOCIAL MARKETING

Millions of potential readers of your book are on a minimum of two social networks. Others are on five or six. You can take advantage of this vast network and talk about your book. Get an account on Twitter and Facebook. Sign up on as many as you can find the time to track. You can even read an excerpt from your book on YouTube.

ONLINE ADVERTISING

Thank heavens for the miracle of technology. The 21st century has tools for advertising that we could not begin to imagine in the 20th century. It is possible to purchase space on the sites of some online booksellers. Check out Paid Placements on Amazon.com.

Don't forget GOOGLE. You can purchase AdWords on search engines that match your book to items that people are searching for on the Internet. These are keywords that when searched will allow your ad to appear next to the search results. This is a great opportunity to advertise to an audience that's already interested in you.

People can click your ad to make a purchase or learn more about you. It is not necessary to have a webpage to get started-Google will help you create one for free.

DIRECT MARKETING

This type of advertisement includes order blanks in books, catalogs, radio, TV, package inserts and direct email. Open the newspapers on certain days and you will find inserts advertising a service or a product. Explore all of these options.

NICHE MARKETING

The days of generalization are gone. Today we have specialization, sometimes called target or niche marketing. People are looking for specifics. They don't have the time or the patience to wade through volumes looking for their exact needs. They want to be able to go straight to the source and zoom in on their focus. Is it fly fishing? Is it doll-making? Is it skydiving? What is it? Whatever it is, they are looking for books on that particular topic. Advertise in your niche market.

DIRECT EMAIL ADVERTISING

In a seminar on Self-publishing, I mentioned to the audience that email advertising is an effective tool. It is surprising how many people overlooked this method of advertising. Even in general, everyday emails, never fail to include an email signature that promotes your book or business. See Chapter 13, page 89 for example of email signature.

It only takes a few minutes to set up your email signature. Go to your email program, click Help and type in *signature*. Follow the instructions. It does not have to be perfect the first time. You will improve it as times goes on.

You Can Be an Author!

15

Fulfillment and Distribution

WOW! The book is done. You are holding a copy in your hand. The question is how to get the book into hundreds or thousands of other hands? How do you get this masterpiece distributed? What about warehousing and shipping and all the other little nit-picking details? Do I have to say it again? Everything you need is out there somewhere. Just a click of the mouse will locate printers that are also fulfillment centers.

What is fulfillment? It consists of all of the processes involved in getting the book out the door including storage of the books, invoicing, packing, and shipping. Is this service expensive? Yes, it is. It has been documented that small to medium-sized publishers spend an inordinate amount on fulfillment, roughly about 10.5 percent. This really cuts into the bottom line of the publisher. If you are self-publishing, you may want to use printers who are also fulfillment centers.

How are you going to sell your books? There are several methods:

ONLINE RETAILERS
Amazon.Com. This is the largest online retail bookseller in the world. If it is in print, you can find it on Amazon. When your book is listed on Amazon, it lends credibility to your book. That's the upside, but what is the downside? Well, Amazon wants a 55 percent discount plus shipping. So by the time you subtract the discount, plus the printing cost (if you are self-publishing), you don't have much left. In addition to that, once Amazon picks up your title, other online retailers will pick it up, too. They undercut Amazon's prices, so Amazon drops the list price to compete.

DEALERS
You can offer your book to local book sellers. Sometimes, it's hard to get into the brick and mortar

stores like Borders and Barnes and Nobles. There is limited shelf space in the stores so only a small percentage of the books from the big publishers end up in the establishment stores. Some of the more visible shelf space is purchased by the publishers. Those books didn't just luck up and end up on the front display.

AFFILIATES

Partner up with somebody. Allow others to sell your books as dealers. Affiliates are popular now. Some of the authors will allow others to sell their books. As a small publisher, I signed up to be an affiliate with a publishing guru because one of his books fits right in with what my clients need. It is a very handy book to offer at seminars or conferences on self-publishing.

POD PUBLISHERS

There are many POD publishers in the marketplace. Before you sign up with any of them, check them out. You need one who can make your book available through wholesalers: Ingram, Baker and Taylor, and online booksellers like Amazon.com and BarnesandNobles.com. Availability to Ingram is important because of the widespread use of the Ingram book database.

WHOLESALERS

Ingram and Baker & Taylor are the two major wholesalers in the United States. While Baker & Taylor is the strongest with libraries, Ingram is the strongest with stores. You need your books made available to both of these wholesalers. They do not have sales representatives; they ship when an order is received.

Ingram. Lightning Source (LSI) is a POD printer that is a subsidiary of Ingram. This is the one I use and I highly recommend them to you. When you sign up with Lightning Source, you serve Ingram through them. The website address for Lightning Source is http://www.lightningsource.com. It is not complicated to use Lightning Source. Simply read and sign their contracts for POD printing and eBook distribution in the United States and the United Kingdom. When you get your ID and password, you are ready to upload your text and cover file to their website.

Baker & Taylor. Replica Books is a POD printer that is a subsidiary of Baker and Taylor. Since they work on an exclusive basis, I did not sign a contract with them. But they purchase from Lightning Source and I am signed up with them. Baker & Taylor likes to deal with out-of-print books.

Independent Book Stores. Unfortunately, many of the independent book stores are struggling. They live in the shadow of Borders, Books a Million, and Barnes and Nobles. Look around your neighborhood. How many independent book stores do you see? I have seen several in my neighborhood rise and fall. It is hard for them to compete against the big chain stores. If you approach them with your book, they will probably ask where they can get it. They do not want to deal with you, but would rather purchase from a wholesaler such as Ingram.

Chain Stores. These are the biggies. They sell at least 25 percent of the books sold in the United States. The Big Three are Books a Million, Borders, and Barnes and Nobles. You have to approach these directly. Contact the book buyers at their headquarters for your category of book.

You Can Be an Author!

16

The Best Kept Secret
in Publishing

Oh, yes, there is a well-kept secret that I am going to reveal to you. You have to promise not to tell anyone else. It has been coined a publishing miracle. Gordon Burgett, the publishing guru, calls it ancillary publishing. You can literally publish your book for free in minutes. What? You want to hear about it?

Well, here goes.

I cannot tell you everything you need to know in these few pages, but I will share the source with you.

As a matter of fact, you can order the information at the end of this book in the Resource section.

You can become a published author very quickly. The miracle is the fact that once you have saved your book in a ready-to-print file, there are seven--you heard me--seven legitimate publishers who will convert your file into a professional-looking book. Two days from submittal to these publishers, your book will be selling worldwide. Do I need to say that again? *Two days from submittal to these publishers, your book will be selling worldwide.*

I know you are dying to know how much it will cost you and if you can possibly take advantage of this miracle. Well, guess what? It will cost you a pauper's penny, almost nothing. E-books are free. Of course, the bound book proof will cost about $30 for overnight shipping to you. When you receive it, read it carefully. Make sure there are no errors.

WHAT IS ANCILLARY PUBLISHING?

Ancillary is defined as auxiliary; subsidiary, supplementary, or secondary. "Ancillary publishers" offer new authors a two-pronged path that gives them the means of publishing without becoming a publisher. It offers established publishers a secondary way of selling books to an audience they would not ordinarily reach.

This is a new way of publishing that opens up multiple markets for you. Visit the Web sites of the Big Seven listed below and learn all about the benefits of submitting your masterpiece to them.

THE BIG SEVEN (UNLIKE THE BIG SIX)

Some of us may never meet muster with the big six publishers located in New York. But we can deal with the big seven located in -wherever. Each one has its unique file requirements. Once your manuscript file is created, there are minor adjustments to meet the criteria for each one of the seven.

Lightning Source (LSI). http://lightningsource.com. This is a Print-on-demand (POD) publisher. They will sell your book in POD format to major distributors such as Ingram. They offer bound and e-books. A bound book will cost $75.00 for set-up and $30 for overnight copy of the bound proof. They provide excellent work and are closely tied to Ingram, a major distributor. Files are submitted as a pdf. Your profit from bound book sales is roughly 30% and 45% for e-book sales.

Create Space. http://www.createspace.com. They supply bound books. Think of CreateSpace as a sort of POD wing that funnels your book into production, then sells them primarily through the www.Amazon.com Web site. Your profit from book sales ranges from 20 - 50%. The file is submitted as a .pdf.

Blurb. http://www.blurb.com. They supply bound books. Books are sold in the Blurb bookstore. Blurb is mostly used for art books or those with lots of photography. You can set your profit 30 to 40 percent above print cost. Files are submitted as a .doc or .pdf.

Lulu. http://www.lulu.com. Lulu provides both bound and e-books. They have their own buyers and some secondary distribution. Your pay will be approximately 22-47% for bound books and 80% for e-books. They will accept .doc files but they prefer pdf.

Kindle. DTP.AMAZON.COM. They offer only e-books for use on the Amazon reader. Your share from sales will be 35%. Read their website for specific details on what kind of files to submit.

Smashwords. http://www.smashwords.com. This is where you send the books if you want to sell to Kindle or iPad. They are a good portal into about eight different digital languages. They supply e-books only. They also sell to a few major houses. Your profit is 85%. They accept .doc files.

Scribd. http://www.scribd.com/ E-books only, primarily documents. Profit is 80%. Most ancillary publishers accept your book in just one format, but Scribd accepts your document 19 different ways. This publishing vehicle is different from the others, but don't dismiss it. Scribd claims to be the largest social publishing company in the world, visited by 60 million viewers a month.

These companies are not charity organizations. They are all in business to make money. How can they make money and publish your book for almost nothing? They offer free production and marketing platforms because they want you to select them to publish your book. They make money when they sell your book to their markets.

The trade off is that you do most of the work at the submission level. You provide a print-ready file, a well-designed cover, sales copy, and your bio. You also must take part in promotional efforts.

IT'S A MIRACLE!

You are almost at the finish line! All you have to do now is get your files in order. You can get detailed information on the submittal of files from their websites. Also, a comprehensive explanation for creating these files is found in Gordon Burgett's *How to Get Your book Published Free in Minutes and Marketed Worldwide in Days.* Go to the link below. http://www.1shoppingcart.com/app/?Clk=3662501

Miracle File #1. Now that you have read your words of wisdom one last time, you are ready to start printing, binding, and selling. The ancillary route is a quick, inexpensive route to multiple markets. The .doc file is accepted by one of the publishers so you are almost ready to publish. That is Miracle File #1.

Miracle File #2. Two of the publishers want a PDF file. What is a PDF file? It is a file format developed by Adobe Systems. PDF stands for Portable Document Format. There is software available that will complete this file conversion for you. Windows 7 has this capability.

Before you convert to PDF, put Miracle File #1 into a folder so it will remain intact. Then you can issue the command for the original file to be converted to a PDF file. When you are satisfied that the PDF file is similar or the same as Miracle File

#1, save it as Miracle File #2 and move it to the same folder as Miracle File #1.

Miracle File #3 and #4. These are easy because they are direct downloads of Files #1 and #2. These are e-book files. E-books are handled by Kindle, Smashwords, LightningSource, Lulu and Scribd.

The first step is to save Miracle File #1 as Miracle File #3. Then make a few changes:

- The front cover becomes the first page. Eliminate any blank pages.

- Remove page numbers in the table of contents, headers, footers, and the index.

- You can take this opportunity to change the font size, but not too big. A 12 or 13 point type is good. If you increase the font size, you may have to insert and delete some earlier page breaks.

- Make chapter and section headings smaller and uniform. This is important if the reader is going to be using a reader such as Kindle.

When all these changes are made, you will need to go back and read the whole book to make sure the contents are exactly what you want the readers to see. Save this streamlined e-book version as Miracle File #3. Put it in the same folder as the other Miracle Files.

Copy the Miracle File #3 as a PDF and call it Master File #4. You may have to make some adjustments because of the page breaks. Files #3 and #4 should be almost identical.

Miracle File #5. This is your cover file. You have two choices. You can have your cover file professionally produced. In this case you will get a .jpg and a .pdf version of your cover which you will submit with your text to the ancillary publishers of your choice.

The second choice is to produce your own cover at the ancillary publisher's Web sites. Make sure your back cover copy is eye-catching and has the WOW! Factor. Whichever of the choices you select, you now have Miracle File #5.

Congratulations! You are ready to publish with seven publishers.

THE NEW WAY OF MARKETING

The book is written and published. Who is going to sell it? Your main goal may have been just seeing your name in print. That's OK, but wouldn't you like to make some money?

There is a new way of marketing and it's not your grandfather's marketing technique. It is a marketing method made available by the ancillary publishers.

There are 23 marketing and promotional tools listed in Gordon's Burgett's book, *"How to Get Your book Published Free in Minutes and Marketed Worldwide in Days."* I will list 10 of them here. If you want to see the other 13, you will have to purchase his book. It is well worth the price. Check the link below:

http://www.1shoppingcart.com/app/?Clk=3662501

Marketing and Promotional Tools

1. **Description.** Tell what your book is about in two super introductions, each self-contained. This should include the purpose, the benefits and what the book is all about and why it is unique. Make one short (100 characters) and one long (750 characters.)

2. **Biography.** What qualifies you to write this book? Convince the reader of your knowledge, experience, skill and uniqueness.

3. **Two Sentence Sales Summary.** Some call this the "elevator speech." Others call it the "30-second commercial." You have just 30 seconds

to sell the benefits of your book. Practice doing this conversationally with a smile.

4. **10-20 Bullet Points.** What are the most compelling contents? Write them down. Then prioritize them in order of interest and benefits.

5. **Website.** This site should complement your book. Include links that make everything accessible. You can pre-sell on your website prior to the book's release.

6. **Squeeze Page.** This short one-link page leads to your shopping cart or to your landing page, which also has one exit, the order form.

7. **Landing Page.** The squeeze page points to this page which sells in greater details and lists all benefits.

8. **Google Presence.** Your ultimate goal is to have as many eyes (hopefully buyers) as possible looking at your website and your book. Keywords strategically placed are the key to successful searches on the Google search engine.

Make sure your book is on the Google book Search database. (See http://books.google.com/support)

9. **The Gadgets.** Ancillary publishers use gadgets such as banners, buttons, or widgets. Use as many of these as you think are appropriate for your marketing campaign. The objective is for the reader to be led to an information and buying source.

10. **Home Market.** These are your friends, relatives, and all those who suffered with you while you were producing your masterpiece. Each one of them should purchase a book and tell all of their friends to do the same.

THIS MIRACLE WAS MADE FOR YOU!

Just think! Your book is being published by not one or two, but seven publishers. The fact that you can publish your book in days instead of months is nothing short of a miracle.

You can submit your book to all seven publishers or you can submit to four or five. That's your choice. The important fact is you will have a book on the market in record time. You do not have to worry about the mechanics of getting the book out. Do what you do best: write. Let the ancillary publishers do what they do best: publish.

Your legacy begins here. Your kids, grandkids, and great-grandkids will be able to read your book. Welcome to the ranks of published authors.

17

Building Your Empire, One
Book at a Time

I became interested in this novel concept after
reading *Empire Building by Writing and Speaking*
by Gordon Burgett. I am highly recommending that
you read this book. Mr. Burgett's premise is that
"each of us knows something that others want to
know or should know." What knowledge do you
possess that can be useful to someone trying to
accomplish what you have already mastered?

Here, we are discussing empire-building as it
pertains to writing books. The writing of the book is

foundational or the beginning of your empire. If you are an expert on any subject and you've written a book on it, why not create more books that are linked to that one.

I recommend another book that talks about spinoff income. It is *The Well-Fed Self-Publisher* by Peter Bowerman. He talks about spinoffs from your book. The book leads to revenue from other sources. For example, one author was getting loads of email about his latest non-fiction, how-to book. After answering hundreds of "mechanics of the business" questions, he decided to start charging a fee for answering questions. It was a one-on-one mentoring service that supplemented the income from the sale of his book.

Books: Your Calling Card. Your book can be the entry into five or six income ventures. Even if you don't sell a lot of books, it can lead you into other revenues that will allow you to earn a full-time living. You can build your empire one book at a time, one venture at a time.

Seminars. Your book can be converted into how-to workshops or seminars. They can be offered through associations. For example, a booklet on *Speak to Impress* was converted to a workshop for students offered through a non-profit organization. At these seminars, the book becomes a part of the back-of-the-room (BOR) sales. Sometimes the books bring in more revenue than the actual speech. But in the long term, the speaking income will surpass the book income.

Teleseminars. Experts can offer teleseminars on their own or be a guest speaker on a sponsored teleseminar. Either way, funds can be earned. The average teleseminar cost around $25.00. Those that are free have products that are offered. The value in those for the speaker is the email/contact list gained from the registrants that can be used for future product offers.

Coaching Program. A good example of this is a popular infomercial on Real Estate Investing. The book was $39.00. After purchasing the book the buyer was later contacted and offered coaching at a cost of $6000. WOW! What a jump in price. Some hourly rates for coaching range from $125 per hour upward to $500 or more. The point is an expert in one topic can expand that topic into a major source of income.

Ezines. Use ezines to raise your profile and build your platform. These online magazines provide information and inspiration with your name on it. It's all about getting your name out there associated with your book. An ezine allows you to capture new buyers and bring them into the fold. Everytime you produce a new product, you have a ready audience to sell to. Provide good information in your ezine and you will have a loyal audience who will eventually become buyers.

E-books. This is almost like "free" money—no books, no inventory, no shipping costs. It's a digital file floating around in cyber space that produces hard, cold cash. There are two categories of e-books:

1. *E-books from hard-copy bound books.* All you have to do is add your cover artwork at the front of your finished file and convert it to a PDF file using Adobe Acrobat®. Presto! You have an ebook.

2. *Stand alone E-books.* Smaller books (200 pages or less) work well as e-books. Be aware that most e-books are not successful because readers haven't caught on to the technology. But they will catch up. It's just a matter of time.

Public Speaking. Your book is your ticket into the lucrative business of public speaking. Sometimes the books comes first, and then the speaking engagements. Sometime it's the other way around. A speaker decides to write a book to expand on his speaking topics. The book then becomes the back-of-the room (BOR) sales. Whatever the order, the real money is in speaking and workshops.

This is really an under-used strategy. Being an author gives you credibility. Use it to your advantage by tapping into that market of public, motivational speaking.

Affiliate Programs. This is a great way to expand your empire. Affiliate programs can be great for making money. As an author, you can recruit others who run sites related to yours, to sell your products on their sites. Likewise, you can sell their products on your site.

If you decide to represent a product make sure it's reputable. Before you agree to allow someone to carry your product make sure they are creditable. Your reputation is too valuable to do any different.

Conferences. Published authors are always invited to share their expertise at writer's conferences. This is another step to building your empire. For a comprehensive list that spans thousands of conferences, check out www.allconferences.com.

The conference does not have to be one related to writing. The author is an expert on the subject of his book. There is a conference where his topic will fit in nicely.

If you truly want to build an empire, one book at a time, the link below provides all the information you need.

http://www.1shoppingcart.com/app/?Clk=4043957

Happy Empire Building!

AFTERWORD

Get set, ready, write!

The world of published authors is not a closed society. **You can be an author!** Making that first step is the hardest part. You can do this.

The experts in the field have saved you from having to re-invent the wheel. Learn from them. Valuable resources are included in the appendix. Remember, any information you need to complete your book-writing project can be found online or in books written by the experts.

Do not read this book and put it down without doing something about bringing your dream to fruition. Procrastination will not get you to the finish line. Action will. Do not wait another minute. Put your shoes on, go to the store, buy the binder, and GET STARTED NOW!

Bettye Knighton

About the Author

With over 30 years experience, **Dr. Bettye W. Knighton** shares her knowledge as a Minister of Christian Education, business executive and entrepreneur through motivational speaking, keynote addresses and team building sessions. The experience of creating ministry groups and businesses from the ground up, uniquely qualifies Dr. Knighton to provide guidance to those who want to achieve growth and success for their churches and organizations. Her journey has been a life-long learning experience that has brought her from the bean-field to the boardroom.

She is owner of Majestically Speaking and CEO/President of Emerge Publishing Group LLC. If there is a book inside you, she can help you publish it. It is her mission to assist others in becoming all that they are ordained to be.

Dr. Knighton is the author of several books. She is a member of Professional Speakers Network, Palm Beach County Life Planners Mastermind Group and International MasterMind Association.

If you need a speaker, consultant, coach or publisher, contact her at:

(561) 601-0349 ~ (561) 863-9554
bettyeknighton@aol.com
www.emergepublishers.com ~ www.bettyespeaks.com

APPENDIX A

Resources

Resources

Books

The following books can be very helpful in producing your literary masterpiece. They can be found in any bookstore or online:

Is there a Book Inside You? Dan Poynter

Writing Non-fiction: Dan Poynter

Niche Publishing, Gordon Burgett

The Well-fed Publisher, Peter Bowman

Empire Building by Writing and Speaking, Gordon Burgett

Self-Publishing for Dummies, Jason Rich

A Writer's Guide to Book Publishing, Richard Balkin

Self-Publishing Manual, Dan Poynter

Online Listings

Sites where you can post your book cover image, blurb, and link for free.

http://reader2.com
www.anobii.com
www.author-network.com
www.authorsden.com
www.bookhitch.com
www.jacketflap.com
www.booksie.com
www.bookswellread.com
www.booktour.com
www.booktribes.com
www.redroom.com
www.writerscafe.org

Articles.
For article outlines and an example of an Article Bank, see
http://parapublishing.com/sites/para/resources/articlebank.cfm
Contribute to Articles.
Subscribe to the following services.
http://www.PRNewswire.com
http://www.ProfNet.com
http://HelpAReporter.com

News Releases. Here are some media distribution services:

http://www.Businesswire.com

Don't forget your local newspapers.

WEB SITES OF INTEREST TO WRITERS

A Cappela Publishing
Lectures, Writing Seminars, books and Tapes
http://www.acappella.com

Allworth Press
Books for the Creative Professional
http://allworth.com

Amazon.com
An online bookstore that has many reviews of the book it sells
http://Amazon.com

Book on Almost Free Publishing
http://www.1shoppingcart.com/app/?Clk=3662501

Bookwire (links to many author websites)
http://www.bookwire.com

Book Zone
http://www.bookzone.com

Children's Writing Resource Center
http://www.write4kids.com/index.html

Communication Unlimited (products for authors
and speakers)
http://www.gordonburgett.com

Dictionary Links
http://www.yahoo.com/reference/dictionaries

Empire Building
http://www.1shoppingcart.com/app/?Clk=4043957

Emerge Publishing Group, LLC
http://www.emergepublishers.com

Inkspot Writer's Forum
http://inkspot.com

Niche Publishing
http://www.1shoppingcart.com/app/?Clk=4043953

Para Publishing
http://www.ParaPublishing.com

The Small Publishers, Artists and Writers Network
http://www.spawn.org

Writers Guild of America
http://www.wga.org/

APPENDIX B

BOOK BUILDING TEMPLATE

A Step-by-Step Guide for Building Your Book

Just Fill-in the Blanks

Book Building Template

Hurray! You've finally decided to get that book written and published. Your first step is to purchase a three-ring binder.

Use this template to make 8.5 x 11 pages to insert into the binder with tabs for front matter, chapters, and back matter. The building process is simple. Just fill in the blanks. It's as simple as painting by numbers.

As you complete information in the binder, transfer the information to your computer. Once the pages are printed, 3-hole punch them and insert them into the binder, replacing the old pages.

For additional information, consult the experts listed in the resource section of the appendix.

Front Cover

You will need someone to design your cover unless you are a gifted designer. Remember, the cover is very important. If it is not effective, your book will never be picked up.

Title:

Subtitle:

Author:

Foreword by:

Testimonials

It is a great idea to send out review copies and obtain **testimonials**. Excerpts from reviews can be placed here. If you have ten to twenty, include two or three on the back cover and the remainder can be placed here.

What others are saying about this book:

Title Page

The title page is on the right-hand side and lists the full title and subtitle of the book. This page may also include the name of the author or editor, the publisher, whether this is an original or revised edition, location of the publisher and the date.

Title:

Subtitle:

Author:

City and State of Publication:

Copyright Page

The copyright page is on the reverse of the title page and is the most critical page in the book. Read it once, read it twice and read it again. All the pertinent information about your book is included on this page. It should be absolutely, positively error-free. You want it to look like a big-time publisher, not a one-book wonder publisher.

List the LCCN, the ISBN, the Cataloging-in-Publication Data (CIP), name and address of the publisher and *printed in the United States of America* or *Printed in Canada* (to avoid export complications).

Each time you revise the book, it is worthwhile to change the copyright page in order to add, for example,
Second Printing, revised, 2011, as this lets the potential purchaser know the book is up to date.

Title:
Subtitle:
Author:
Published by:
(Your company name and address):

Dedication Page

The dedication page. You may want to praise your greatest supporters on this page. Historically, this page was used by writers to acknowledge those who supported them financially while they wrote.

For

Epigraph

This page contains a single quote that is pertinent to the contents of the book. This is a nice touch but is not necessary.

Table of Contents

The table of contents should start on the right-hand side. This page will include the chapter numbers, chapter titles and beginning page numbers. Don't be concerned about the page numbers right now. When you have completed the manuscript you can go back and fill in the page numbers. Your book can have any number of chapters. If you plan on having more than ten chapters, just add additional pages.

Table of Contents

Chapter One

Chapter Two

Chapter Three

Chapter Four

Chapter Five

Chapter Six

Chapter Seven

Chapter Eight

Chapter Nine

Chapter Ten

About the Author

About the Author

Draft a page about you as it pertains to the subject matter in this book. If you prefer, you may place this page at the end of the book. Placement of this information is entirely up to you. Include your picture.

Photo of you

Foreword

The foreword is always positioned on the right hand side. It is written by someone other than the author. Get someone in the field about which you are writing. It should be someone who is an expert in the field or someone with great name recognition. Please note the correct spelling. It is not "forword" .

It is not absolutely necessary to have a foreword. Most people don't read them anyway. They want to get right to the action.

Acknowledgement

Acknowledgments are valuable as a sales tool. Everyone wants to see his name in print. Be sure and include anybody who had anything to do with your book.

Chapter One

Title:

Chapter Two

Title:

Chapter Three

Title:

Chapter Four

Title:

Chapter Five

Title:

Chapter Six

Title:

Chapter Seven

Title:

Chapter Eight

Title:

Chapter Nine

Title:

Chapter Ten

Title:

Appendix

The appendix contains important lists and other resources; it may be composed of several sections. As you collect information on your subject, add resources to this section. Add other books, reports, associations, conferences, tapes, suppliers and so on. A book with a large appendix often becomes a valuable reference that people have to own.

To save space, print just the company name and their URL. Area Codes and other address info change too often. It is permissible to set this reference material in smaller type.

Resources

Bibliography

The bibliography lists the reference materials or sources used in writing the book.

Index

The index aids the reader in locating specific information in the pages and is particularly important in reference works. Many librarians will not purchase books without indexes, so plan on including an index. The index is at the very end of the book to make it easy to locate.

You can assemble an index with your word processing program. Read through your typeset manuscript and list the key words and the page numbers. List all the main headings, subheadings and words readers might look for. Double post two-word listings ("bridge building") and ("building, bridge"), and cross-reference different terms. Format the page in two columns, and set the type in ragged-right alignment. Then use your computer to *AutoSort* the list. The index must be revised every time the book is updated if the page numbers change.

Order Blank

Order blank. This is optional. If you decide to include it, it should be the last page in the book. If you have one extra page, the order blank should be on the left-hand page facing out. If you have two free pages it can be on the right facing the reader. It should contain all of the products available for sale. List the full price of products including sales tax (if applicable) and shipping. It is easier to get PayPal for a credit card than a bank card.

QUICK ORDER FORM
Satisfaction Guaranteed

❑ **Email orders:** @

❑ **Fax orders:**   ( ) . Send this form.

❑ **Telephone orders:** Call 1 ( )
Have your credit card ready.

❑ Postal orders:

Please send the following Books, Discs or Courses. I understand that I may return any of them for a full refund-for any reason, no questions asked.

Name:
Address:
City, State/Province, Postal Code

Tel:
Email:
Sales tax:
Shipping by air:
Payment: PayPal

www.yourwebsiteaddress

Book Covers Work Sheet

FRONT COVER

SPINE

BACK COVER

APPENDIX C

NonFiction Book
Proposal Outline

Nonfiction Book Proposal Outline

I.   Overview

Describe your book in two or three paragraphs (500 words or less). What is the title and subtitle? Who is the target audience and what makes your book unique? Think of this as the back-cover blurb or the ad in the publisher's catalog. Also, you can use this to put into the Publishers Weekly or the New York Times Review.

II.   Target Audience

Who is your target audience, the most likely purchasers of this book? What other groups and types of readers will also be interested in your book?

III.   About the Author

What are your credentials and experience? What makes you uniquely qualified to write and promote this book? Do you regularly appear in any other media outlets?

IV.   Competitive Titles

Search the Internet for those titles in your category. List and summarize the major competitive titles and explain why yours is different from each. In this section you are trying to prove there is an audience who would find your book interesting. Stress why readers should buy your book.

V.   Marketing and Promotion

What is your comprehensive plan to actively promote the book? Will you make effective use of the Internet to market your book? Where should publicity be focused? What are the magazines and other media outlets that your target audience pays attention to? Where should you and your publisher work especially hard too get the book reviewed?

VI.   Table of Contents

Include the full Table of Contents, with detailed summaries of each chapter. This section could be anywhere from three to 20 pages. This section needs to give a comprehensive, detailed map of what the book will contain.

VII. Sample Chapters

Include the first one or two chapters-not the introduction. The chapters included in the proposal should offer an accurate sense of the style, substance, and structure of the book.

INDEX

www.ingramcontent.com/pod-product-compliance
Lightning Source LLC
Chambersburg PA
CBHW060853280326
41934CB00007B/1031